WHERE THE SAVIOR LEADS

Where *the* Savior Leads

31 DAILY MEDITATIONS *on* FOLLOWING JESUS

BILLY GRAHAM

Compiled from Decision *magazine*

BILLY GRAHAM EVANGELISTIC ASSOCIATION

Charlotte, North Carolina

Table *of* Contents

Where the Savior Leads

All Scripture quotations, unless otherwise indicated, are taken from The Holy Bible, English Standard Version, ©2001 by Crossway Bibles, a publishing ministry of Good News Publishers. Used by permission. All rights reserved.

Scripture quotations marked NKJV are taken from the New King James Version. ©1982 by Thomas Nelson, Inc. Used by permission. All rights reserved.

Scripture quotations marked NIV are taken from the Holy Bible, New International Version. ©1973, 1978, 1984, 2011 by Biblica, Inc. Used by permission. All rights reserved worldwide.

Scripture quotations marked GW are taken from GOD'S WORD, ©1995 God's Word to the Nations. Used by permission of Baker Publishing Group.

These devotions are edited excerpts from articles published in *Decision* magazine. Used by permission.

ISBN: 978-1-59328-416-9

Foreword

My father's life is a wonderful example of what God can do when a person follows Jesus Christ faithfully. From the time he gave his life to Jesus as a teenager, he sought God's leading. Through his ministry, millions of people around the world have heard the Good News of the Savior who loves them unconditionally.

For this devotional book, we've selected 31 excerpts from his articles published in *Decision* magazine. Each one offers a reminder of what it means to follow Christ and how He can guide the choices we make. I pray that these readings will help you to experience the joy and hope that can be found when we choose the path that leads to everlasting life.

We would appreciate hearing if you find this book helpful in your walk with Christ or if you have been touched by the ministry of the Billy Graham Evangelistic Association in other ways. To contact us, or to learn more about our ministry, see the information on the last page. May God richly bless you.

Franklin Graham
November 2013

Though you have not seen him, you love him. Though you do not now see him, you believe in him and rejoice with joy that is inexpressible and filled with glory, obtaining the outcome of your faith, the salvation of your souls. —1 PETER 1:8–9

What *is a* Christian?

In many parts of the world there is a spiritual and a moral vacuum. Millions of people seem to have no purpose for living, no motivating challenge. People are restless. They want a cause. They want a flag to follow. Jesus Christ doesn't call us to be bystanders or spectators. The word "Christian" actually means "a partisan for Christ." It means that we have chosen Christ and we are following Christ. Partisans are not neutral.

Many people have a wrong idea of what a Christian is. They say, "A Christian is a person who prays." Christians do pray, but prayer doesn't make someone a Christian. Or, "A Christian lives by the Golden Rule." But living by the Golden Rule doesn't make someone a Christian.

A person may be sincere, but that doesn't make him a Christian. When I was a little boy, my mother was sincere when she gave me what she thought was cough syrup for my cold. She had instead given me iodine. She quickly called the doctor, and he said, "Give him some cream." We had a little dairy farm with about sixty cows, and she almost filled me up with cream.

Some people think that a Christian is one who tries to keep the Ten Commandments. Everyone has broken the Ten Commandments. The Bible says that if we break one commandment, we are guilty of breaking them all. So we have broken the whole of the Ten Commandments, and in the Bible that is called "sin."

Some people say, "A Christian is a person who goes to church." Yes, a Christian ought to go to church, but attending church doesn't make someone a Christian.

A Christian is someone who has a real, genuine, personal relationship with Jesus Christ.

Prayer *for the* Day:

Heavenly Father, following Jesus gives me a purpose for living instead of the emptiness seen in those around me. Thank You for sending Your Son to earth, so that I might have a personal relationship with Him.

Day 2

There is salvation in no one else, for there is no other name
under heaven ... by which we must be saved. —ACTS 4:12

The Only Way

Why is Christianity so different from every other religion in the world?

The answer focuses not on a plan for living, but on the Person of Jesus Christ: Jesus, the Son of God the Father and the Second Person of the Trinity.

Today many voices are making other claims. Atheism says there is no God. Polytheism says Jesus is one of many gods. But we boldly echo the ringing conviction of the Apostle Peter: *"You are the Christ, the Son of the living God"* (Matthew 16:16).

The title "Christ" means "anointed one." It is the term, in the Greek language, for the ancient Hebrew word "Messiah"—the "anointed one" whom God would send to save His people. Peter and the first believers of the early Christian church recognized Jesus as the Messiah promised in the Old Testament. He is *"the Lamb of God, who takes away the sin of the world!"* (John 1:29). He is the hope of the hopeless and the helpless.

Their period of world history was one of discouragement and despair. The promised Messiah shone as a beacon in the darkness, and His light has never dimmed: *"In him was life, and the life was the light of men. ... The true light, which gives light to everyone, was coming into the world"* (John 1:4, 9).

Today, as world leaders struggle with seemingly insurmountable problems, as storm clouds gather around the globe, this darkening and menacing situation accentuates the brightness of the One who proclaimed, *"I am the light of the world. Whoever follows me will not walk in darkness, but will have the light of life"* (John 8:12).

Prayer *for the* Day:

I believe that You, Jesus, are the only One who can save me, who can give me life. You are my hope when I feel hopeless and my light in the midst of darkness. Shine Your light through me to those around me.

Now therefore fear the Lord and serve him in sincerity and in faithfulness. Put away the gods that your fathers served beyond the River and in Egypt, and serve the Lord. And if it is evil in your eyes to serve the Lord, choose this day whom you will serve. ... But as for me and my house, we will serve the Lord.
—JOSHUA 24:14–15

Choosing Your Road

A Christian is a person who has made a choice. All the way through the Bible we are asked to make choices. In the Garden of Eden, Adam and Eve made the wrong choice. They chose to rebel against God, and then they chose to try to build their world without God. They made a terrible, tragic mistake. Our first parents broke God's Law and passed on the results of their disobedience to their children, and they have passed on the results to you and to me.

We are all capable of sin, and we all do sin. David said, "*Indeed, I was born guilty. I was a sinner when my mother conceived me*" (Psalm 51:5, GW). We were born in sin. We are sinners by choice. We are sinners by practice.

Jesus said that only a few people are on the narrow road that leads to Heaven. The vast majority are on a broad road that leads to judgment, destruction and hell.

It is what we do about Jesus Christ, His death on the cross and His resurrection that counts. If we enter that narrow gate at the cross and the resurrection and say, "Yes, Lord, I believe; I turn from my sins; I'm willing to change my way of living," we will walk on the narrow road that may be rocky and rough and difficult. But at the end of that road will be Heaven. On that road God gives us new resources, a new power, a new joy and a new love.

Prayer *for the* Day:

Lord, I believe that You died for my sins. I have chosen to follow You today and every day for as long as I live. Each day, give me Your strength for the journey.

And calling the crowd to him with his disciples, [Jesus] said to them, "If anyone would come after me, let him deny himself and take up his cross and follow me. For whoever would save his life will lose it, but whoever loses his life for my sake and the gospel's will save it." —MARK 8:34–35

No Compromise

Some people refuse Christ because of the church. They say, "Churches are full of hypocrites." But there are hypocrites in every area of life. The church is for sinners, saved by the grace of God. In my own power I'm not worthy to be a member of the Body of Christ. But Christ Himself founded the church, and its purpose is to glorify God.

I think the main reason that people don't come to Christ is that they don't want to pay the price. Christ will not compromise. He will not negotiate. We come by repentance and faith, or we don't come at all.

Jesus said, *"For what does it profit a man to gain the whole world and forfeit his soul?"* (Mark 8:36). Suppose you had all the wealth in the entire world and lost your soul. Would it be worth it?

Your soul is that part of you that will live forever. The decision that you make about Jesus Christ is your soul's eternal destiny. Some people put off that decision. But the Bible says, *"Behold, now is the accepted time; behold, now is the day of salvation"* (2 Corinthians 6:2, NKJV). And, *"He who is often reproved, yet stiffens his neck, will suddenly be broken beyond healing"* (Proverbs 29:1).

What do you have to do? You have to be willing to say, "God, I'm a sinner." That is repentance. You have to be willing to turn from sin. Then by faith you have to commit your life to Christ and put Him first from now on.

If you haven't already, won't you make that choice right now?

Prayer *for the* Day:

Dear God, I know I'm a sinner. I'm sorry for my sins, and I choose to turn from sin and follow Jesus. I commit my life to Jesus Christ.

Note: If you have accepted Jesus Christ as Savior and you need help in understanding your decision, turn to page 64.

For there is one God, and there is one mediator between God and men, the man Christ Jesus. —1 TIMOTHY 2:5

Truth Does Not Change

In all my evangelistic ministry I never felt a need to "adapt" Jesus to the many and varied nationalities, cultures, tribes or ethnic groups to whom I have preached. I tried instead to adapt illustrations or to emphasize certain truths that would help a particular audience understand the Gospel more clearly in light of their cultural background.

The essential truths of the Gospel do not change. The facts concerning His virgin birth, His sinless life, His sacrificial and substitutionary death, His resurrection and ascension to the right hand of the Father, and the glorious hope of His Return must not be diluted or distorted in any way.

Jesus is not only the Christ; He is also God, "our Lord and Savior." This is a staggering, almost incomprehensible truth: God Himself has come down on this planet in the Person of

His only Son. This great truth is underlined throughout the New Testament. John begins his Gospel, *"In the beginning was the Word"* (John 1:1). The word "logos" in Greek, translated "word," would have been understood by Hebrews and Greeks alike. Then John continues, *"And the Word was with God, and the Word was God. … And the Word became flesh and dwelt among us, and we have seen his glory, glory as of the only Son from the Father, full of grace and truth"* (John 1:1, 14).

The incarnation and the full deity of Jesus are the cornerstones of the Christian faith. Jesus Christ was not just a great teacher or a holy religious leader. He was God in human flesh—fully God and fully man. That truth is timeless.

Prayer *for the* Day:

Dear God, You never change. Your truth is the same today as it has always been. Please reveal Yourself and Your truth through my life to those around me.

Day 6

Therefore, if anyone is in Christ, he is a new creation. The old has passed away; behold, the new has come. —2 CORINTHIANS 5:17

Has *your* Life *been* Transformed?

A Christian's life has been changed by the Holy Spirit. The moment we receive Jesus Christ, the Spirit of God comes to live in our hearts. Christ gives us a new heart.

People are changed by the renewing of their minds. We act the way that we believe. Our changing from being defeated, problem-oriented people depends on our changing our minds. When you change your mind about God, about Christ, and follow Him, you find the peace and satisfaction that only He gives.

Our problems, our emotional upsets, our feelings, our behavior and our goals are rooted in our personal needs in life. Christ can take charge of our problems, if we let Him.

11

Jesus said, *"Whoever wants to be my disciple must deny themselves and take up their cross and follow me"* (Matthew 16:24, NIV). In other words, we deny self—our own selfish ambitions, our own sinful pleasures; then we take up our cross. What did Jesus mean by that? He is saying that when you go back to your neighborhood, back to your work and tell people that you have received Christ, they may laugh at you. They may make fun of you. Maybe your peers and your friends will no longer have anything to do with you. You may have to pay a price.

Jesus paid a high price. Many of the people who followed Jesus quit following Him when He talked about death. They didn't understand the deeper meaning of His death and resurrection. They didn't realize that when He died on the cross and rose again, that was their only hope to have their sins forgiven and to get to Heaven.

Whatever the cost to follow Jesus, the new heart He gives is worth it. Christ is the only hope that we have in this life or in the life to come.

Prayer *for the* Day:

Dear Jesus, thank You for the hope You give me. I give You my problems, my hurts, my selfish desires, and I ask that You give me Your peace and satisfaction.

I will give you a new heart, and a new spirit I will put within you. —EZEKIEL 36:26

New Heart, New Beginning

A newspaper article some time ago carried a headline that said, "A new world is being born." Jesus said that it is possible to live a new life. He said, *"You must be born again"* (John 3:7).

Jesus talked with Nicodemus, a religious ruler who was a rich Pharisee. Pharisees were considered the leaders of the country, and Nicodemus belonged to the Sanhedrin, the highest ruling body in the nation. Jesus told Nicodemus, "If you are not born again, you will never see the Kingdom of God" (see John 3:3).

Nicodemus was the kind of person whom most churches would be glad to have as a member. But Jesus said, "Nicodemus, all your good works and all your religious knowledge is not enough. You need something more." Jesus knew that all of us are capable of lying and cheating and hate and prejudice and social inequality. He said, *"For out of the heart come evil thoughts, murder, adultery, sexual immorality, theft, false witness, slander. These are what defile a person"* (Matthew 15:19–20).

What is the new birth? What does it mean to start over? Nicodemus asked, *"How can a man be born when he is old?"* (John 3:4). He wanted to understand it. But Jesus indicated to him that there's a mystery about it: *"Born, not of blood nor of the will of the flesh nor of the will of man, but of God"* (John 1:13).

To be born again means to be *"born from above"* (John 3:7, GW). The Holy Spirit of God comes in and gives us a new heart.

Prayer *for the* Day:

Your Holy Spirit has given me a new heart, and I praise You for making me a new person. Continue to mold me into the person You want me to be.

Enter by the narrow gate. For the gate is wide and the way is easy that leads to destruction, and those who enter by it are many. For the gate is narrow and the way is hard that leads to life, and those who find it are few. —MATTHEW 7:13–14

Two Roads *in* Life

Jesus plainly stated that there are two roads in life. One is broad—lacking in faith, convictions and morals. It is the easy, popular, careless way. It is the way of the crowd, the way of the majority, the way of the world. Jesus said, *"Those who enter by it are many"* (Matthew 7:13). But that road, easy though it is, popular though it is, heavily traveled though it is, leads to destruction. And in loving, compassionate intolerance Jesus said, *"Enter by the narrow gate. ... For the gate is narrow and the way is hard that leads to life"* (Matthew 7:13–14).

Jesus spoke of two roads, two kingdoms, two masters, two rewards and two eternities. And He said, *"I am the way, and the* truth, and the life. No one comes to the Father except through me" (John 14:6). We have the power to choose whom we will serve, but the alternative to choosing Christ brings certain destruction. Jesus said that! The broad, wide, easy, popular way leads to death and destruction. Only the way of the cross leads Home.

A person who has a popular, tolerant attitude toward the Gospel of Jesus Christ is like a person watching a baseball game and rooting for both teams. It would be impossible for an individual who has no loyalty to a particular team to be excited about the game.

Jesus said, *"No one can serve two masters, for either he will hate the one and love the other, or he will be devoted to the one and despise the other. You cannot serve God and money"* (Matthew 6:24). One of the sins of this age is the sin of broad-mindedness. We need more people who will step out and say unashamedly, *"As for me and my house, we will serve the Lord"* (Joshua 24:15).

Prayer *for the* Day:

God, help me to be unashamed that I have chosen to serve You. When I am tempted to divide my loyalties, remind me of Your unfailing love and help me to remain on the path You have provided that leads to life.

Day 9

Simon Peter replied, "You are the Christ, the Son of the living God." —MATTHEW 16:16

Neutral *is* Not *an* Option

Some people resist the idea of a choice of any sort. They don't want to be called "narrow." But Jesus taught that there are two roads, and that we have to choose which road we will take. There are two masters, and we have to choose which master we will serve. There are two destinies: Heaven and hell. We have to make a choice.

God doesn't make the choice for us. He helps us to make the choice by sending His Holy Spirit to convict us. But ultimately we make our own choice. God gave us the gift of free will. We can say, "I will," or, "I won't." Which will it be for you? Jesus does not allow us to be neutral about Him. Jesus demands that we decide.

In Matthew 16, Jesus asked His disciples, "Who do you say that I am?"

Peter answered, "You are the Christ, the Son of the living God."
And Jesus said, "Peter, you are right."

The Bible says, *"God is love"* (1 John 4:8). He loves you. He is interested in you. He has the hairs of your head numbered (see Matthew 10:30). He loves you *"with an everlasting love"* (Jeremiah 31:3). And He wants to forgive you. He wants to come into your life and into your home and into your work and into all of your relationships and help you. But He does not come without an invitation.

Some people are reluctant to make that choice because they are not sure that anyone can prove God. No one can prove God. We can't go to a scientific laboratory and say, "Here is God in a test tube." We accept God by faith.

Prayer *for the* Day:

God, Your love overwhelms me. Your Holy Spirit convicts me. And I choose to believe that Jesus is the Christ, Your Son. Work in my life and in my home and in all my relationships as I seek to live for You.

All Scripture is breathed out by God and profitable for teaching, for reproof, for correction, and for training in righteousness. —2 TIMOTHY 3:16

You Can Depend *on the* Bible

S ome people raise questions about the Bible, such as, "Can we trust the Bible?" But the Scripture says, *"All scripture is given by inspiration of God"* (2 Timothy 3:16, NKJV).

The written Word of God was prepared under the direction of the Holy Spirit: *"No prophecy of Scripture comes from someone's own interpretation. For no prophecy was ever produced by the will of man, but men spoke from God as they were carried along by the Holy Spirit"* (2 Peter 1:20–21). Even though the human writers of Scripture wrote as people of their time, God ensured that the words and thoughts were inspired and recorded accurately as He intended.

Because the Bible is God's inspired Word, it does not

contradict itself or teach falsehoods—because God cannot lie. We may not understand every detail of Scripture, but we must never lose sight of the fact that it is God's Word and not man's ideas or opinions.

I don't understand everything in the Bible. I accept the Bible by faith as the Word of God. It has changed my life, and it feeds my soul. Every time I read the Bible, it speaks to me.

Job said, *"I have treasured the words of his [God's] mouth more than my portion of food"* (Job 23:12). The Bible is a living Book, a Book about faith, a Book about God. It is a living Book that speaks to us as we read it.

Prayer *for the* Day:

The Bible says Your Word is truth. Use it, dear God, to teach me and to show me how to live a life pleasing to You.

Day 11

So shall my word be that goes out from my mouth; it shall not return to me empty, but it shall accomplish that which I purpose, and shall succeed in the thing for which I sent it.
—ISAIAH 55:11

The Word Has Power

Jesus constantly quoted the Old Testament and made it clear that it was the inspired Word of God. We who follow Christ must have just as high a view of Scripture as Jesus did. The Word of God has the power to change lives. (See 1 Corinthians 2:4–5.)

God has promised to bless His Word. Time after time in my ministry I have quoted a Bible verse in a sermon—sometimes without planning to do so in advance—and afterward someone has told me it was that verse which the Holy Spirit used to bring conviction or faith: *"Is not my word like fire, declares the Lord, and like a hammer that breaks the rock in pieces?"* (Jeremiah 23:29).

One moonlit night in the mountains of California I went out alone with my Bible. I laid my open Bible on the stump of a tree and prayed, "O Lord, I don't understand everything in this Book, but I accept it by faith as the Word of the living God." Since that moment I've never doubted that the Bible is the Word of God. God has confirmed this to me, as I have witnessed the power of the Word of God at work in the lives of people.

Our call and power come from the infallible Word of God— the Bible. It is the very Scripture in which Jesus is revealed. Him we believe; Him we trust; Him we proclaim as Savior; Him we confess before others as our Lord. He is the same yesterday, today and forever (see Hebrews 13:8).

That is the foundation of the truth we declare. That is why we rejoice!

Prayer *for the* Day:

I rejoice today, Lord, that You reveal Yourself to us through the Bible. I am grateful that Your Word has the power to change the lives of others as it has changed mine.

By him all things were created. ... And he is before all things, and in him all things hold together. —COLOSSIANS 1:16–17

He *is who* He Said

What proof did Jesus offer that He was truly God in human form?

There was the proof of His perfect life. He asked, *"Can any of you prove me guilty of sin?"* (John 8:46, NIV)—and no one could answer because His life was perfect. He was blameless. *"In every respect [He] has been tempted as we are, yet without sin"* (Hebrews 4:15).

There was the evidence of His power—the power of God almighty. He quieted the storms, raised the dead, healed the sick, restored sight to the blind, and made the lame walk. His miracles were a witness to the fact that He is Lord of all nature.

There was the evidence of fulfilled prophecy. Hundreds of years before His birth, the prophets of the Old Testament spoke precisely of the place where He would be born (Micah 5:2) and of the manner of His death and burial (Psalm 22, Isaiah 53). Uncounted details of His life were foretold by the prophets, and every prophecy was fulfilled.

There was the evidence of His resurrection. Jesus Christ *"was declared to be the Son of God in power ... by his resurrection from the dead"* (Romans 1:4). The founders of non-Christian religions of the world have died and been buried. But Christ is alive! His resurrection is a fact! His tomb is empty.

Then there is the proof of changed lives. Christ alone, the divine Son of God, has power to change the human heart. And He does. The Bible says, *"If anyone is in Christ, he is a new creation"* (2 Corinthians 5:17).

Yes, Jesus Christ is who He said He is: God Himself in human form. Only the risen and ascended Son of God is worthy of our worship and our service.

Prayer *for the* Day:

You are worthy, Lord Jesus, of my worship and my service. Show me today how You would have me live, so that others might see You and know that You are God.

Day 13

The wind blows where it wishes, and you hear its sound, but you do not know where it comes from or where it goes. So it is with everyone who is born of the Spirit. —JOHN 3:8

Dye *on* Our Souls

A man pulled a gun on a bank teller and instructed the teller to hand him the money inside a bag. But the man did not know that the bag also contained a dye bomb. When the bomb exploded, it covered the money, the bag and his hand with dye. He couldn't get the dye off. The police caught him because the dye was easy to see.

Because of sin, we have "dye" on our souls, and we can't wash off the stain. But Jesus can cleanse our stains with His blood. The only way to cleanse the stain of sin is by the blood of Christ: *"The blood of Jesus his [God's] Son cleanses us from all sin"* (1 John 1:7). And that's what we need.

When we receive Christ, He comes to dwell in us. He will live in us. We can't live a Christian life by ourselves. We need to have the Holy Spirit living in us to help us live the Christian life. I couldn't live the Christian life for one hour without the work of the Holy Spirit. I'm a sinner saved by the grace of God.

One of the Jewish rulers, a man named Nicodemus, asked Jesus, "How can it happen?" (see John 3:4). Jesus said that it is a mystery. He used the analogy of the wind. He said, "The wind blows wherever it pleases. You can't see it, you can't catch it, but you can feel it. You can see the effects of it" (see John 3:8). The Holy Spirit comes into our hearts and gives us a new nature. We can't pick it up and analyze it with our hands or inspect it in a laboratory. It is the work of the Spirit of God in us, when we say "yes" to Christ.

Prayer *for the* Day:

Dear Jesus, I don't understand it and I can't see it, but I know that the Holy Spirit lives in me, because I have accepted You as my Savior. I praise You because You have given me a new heart and a new nature and removed the stain of sin.

All we like sheep have gone astray; we have turned—every one—to his own way; and the Lord has laid on him the iniquity of us all.
—ISAIAH 53:6

Two Greatest Words

I saw a 106-year-old woman interviewed on television, and I wondered how many people will live to be 106 years old. Not many. So we don't have much time. Our time is very short. It is brief. We will soon be dead and gone.

The Bible describes sins that we commit as free acts of intelligent, moral, responsible beings. There are many words in the Bible that are equated with "sin." "Transgression" is one of them. Transgression of the Law means that we have broken the Ten Commandments. Every person has broken the Ten Commandments, and the Bible says that if we have broken even one Commandment, we are guilty of having broken them all (see James 2:10). That means that we have broken all of the Commandments. And we haven't lived up to the principles in the Sermon on the Mount. We miss the mark. *"All wrongdoing is sin"* (1 John 5:17), the Scripture says.

Then there is "iniquity." Iniquity means a turning aside from the straight path: *"All we like sheep have gone astray; we have turned—every one—to his own way"* (Isaiah 53:6). The Bible teaches that the spirit is dead toward God. We all have bodies, but living inside is our spirit; and it is our spirit that will live forever either in Heaven or in hell. The destination will be determined by the decision that we make about Jesus Christ.

Probably the two greatest words in the English language are "Not guilty." And that's what God will say to you at the Judgment, if you know Christ.

Prayer *for the* Day:

Dear God, I know that I am a sinner, but I thank You for rescuing me from my sins and putting me on Your path. When I stray, You bring me back. But help me not to stray from Your will.

Day 15

Jesus said ... , "When you have lifted up the Son of Man, then you will know that I am he." —JOHN 8:28

What *is* Truth?

Many people today are asking, "What is truth?" The Bible tells the truth. It tells the truth about God, about man, about the devil. Inside the Bible are stories of lust and hate and war and crime equal to anything that we read about in history.

Jesus Christ told the truth about sin. He said, *"Out of the heart come evil thoughts, murder, adultery, sexual immorality, theft, false witness, slander"* (Matthew 15:19) and all other sins that we commit. War comes from the human heart. Family tensions and problems come from the human heart. Rebellion comes from the human heart.

He told the truth about love. God loves you. And He loves you with a love that you don't know anything about, because there is no human love comparable to divine love. God's love sent His

Son to the cross to die and shed His blood for you. He would have died had you been the only person in the whole world.

Jesus told the truth about judgment. He warned people to "flee the wrath of God" (see Matthew 3:7). Yes, God is angry with the wicked. Jesus said, *"I tell you, on the day of judgment people will give account for every careless word they speak"* (Matthew 12:36). Every idle word, all your thoughts, all your words, everything you have ever done, will be at the Judgment. And you will be condemned by your own words.

Jesus said, *"Unless you believe that I am he you will die in your sins"* (John 8:24). If people don't believe that and don't accept Christ, they will die in their sins and be lost. Jesus Christ claimed to be ultimate truth. Are you willing to share the truth with those who don't know Him?

Prayer *for the* Day:

Lord, I believe that You died for me, but You also died for my family and my friends. Open my eyes to opportunities to share the truth of Your love with others today.

They exchanged the truth about God for a lie and worshiped and served the creature rather than the Creator, who is blessed forever! —ROMANS 1:25

Truth *or* Lies?

T he first time that man had to make a choice between God's truth and the devil's lie, He chose the devil's lie. When Adam and Eve rejected God's truth and accepted the devil's lie, in that moment all the troubles of the whole world began. Our sinful nature often sides with the devil's lie instead of God's truth, because we are sinners.

To those involved in this dying world Satan will come with evil's undiluted power to deceive, for they have refused the truth which could have saved them. God sends upon them, therefore, the full force of evil's delusion, so that they put their faith in an utter fraud and meet the inevitable judgment of all who have refused to believe the truth and who have made evil their playfellow (see 2 Thessalonians 2:9–12). God says these people deliberately forfeited the truth of God and accepted a lie. God, therefore, handed them over to disgraceful passions (see Romans 1:24–26). They see truth as a lie and the lie as the truth. They accept the lies of the devil.

We find deception, delusion and the practicing of the lie on every hand. The credibility gap is everywhere. What is the answer? What can people do? Turn to Christ; turn to the truth. Jesus said, *"You will know the truth, and the truth will set you free"* (John 8:32). He said, *"I am ... the truth* (John 14:6). Jesus did not say, "You shall know a truth," or "any truth," but *the* truth. He's the embodiment of all truth.

Prayer *for the* Day:

It is so easy, Jesus, for me to be deceived, but I believe that You are the truth. Make me aware of Satan's attempts to deceive, and give me Your power to discern and defeat his attacks.

Day 17

*Jesus answered him, "Truly, truly, I say to you, unless one is born again he cannot see the kingdom of God." —*JOHN 3:3

Like Little Children

Jesus told the truth about repentance. He said, *"Unless you repent, you will all likewise perish"* (Luke 13:3). Repentance means change. I change my mind about God, about myself, about my fellow man. I change my way of living. But on my own I don't have strength to change. I can't change. I can't become a Christian. Why? Because I'm *"dead in [my] trespasses and sins"* (Ephesians 2:1). God has to help me change. He has to help me repent. And I have to say, "O God, help me to repent."

Not only do we have to repent, but by faith we must receive Christ into our hearts as Savior and Lord. Jesus told the truth about conversion. He said we have to be born from above, born again (see John 3:3). Jesus said, *"Unless you turn and become like children, you will never enter the kingdom of heaven"*

(Matthew 18:3). In other words, He's not telling people to become like adults. He's telling us to become like little children and have childlike faith.

Some people try to enter the Kingdom of God head first. They want to understand it, but we can never comprehend it all. There are many things in the Bible I don't understand. We come by simple faith, like a little child who trusts his mother and father. We put our total confidence in Jesus Christ by faith.

Repent, receive by faith and then obey Him. Live the life. Follow Him, serve Him whatever the cost. And it is costly. In the world in which we live, if we hold on to Christian values and live up to moral standards laid down by Christ, it will cost us. Are you willing to do that?

Prayer *for the* Day:

Dear God, I don't understand everything the Bible says, but I put my trust in Jesus Christ. Help me to live a life that is pleasing to You, regardless of the cost.

What does it profit a man to gain the whole world and forfeit his soul? For what can a man give in return for his soul?
—MARK 8:36–37

Obstacles *to* Jesus

As Jesus went through Jericho, a crowd gathered around Him. There was a short man in the crowd named Zacchaeus. He wanted to see Jesus, but he couldn't see over the heads of the people. So he ran to a sycamore tree, and he climbed up to gain some height.

Zacchaeus faced a lot of obstacles to get to Jesus. First, there was the press of the crowd. And he was a short man. You too have obstacles in coming to Jesus. Your obstacle may be pride. You are afraid of what people will say. Or you say, "I'm a church member. I'm a good person. I own a Bible." Many people have Bibles in their homes, but they don't read them, they don't study them. They are ignorant of the Bible.

Another obstacle for you might be love of the world. People

have told me, "I hope that Jesus doesn't come for a long time. I'd hate to have to leave."

"What good is it for someone to gain the whole world," asked Jesus, "yet forfeit their soul? Or what can anyone give in exchange for their soul?"

We cannot escape being in the world, but we don't have to be of the world. We don't need to partake of the world's evil things. We don't need to think the way the world thinks. We will be judged not only on what we do but on what we think as well.

"Man looks at the outward appearance, but the Lord looks at the heart" (1 Samuel 16:7, NKJV), the Scripture says.

Prayer *for the* Day:

Jesus, sometimes I do let pride or love of the world become an obstacle to following You. Replace my heart with Yours so that I might be faithful to Your calling in my life.

The sheep hear his voice; and he calls his own sheep by name and leads them out. —JOHN 10:3

He Calls Us *by* Name

The man named Zacchaeus was up in a sycamore tree, and Jesus was passing the tree. Jesus looked up, and said, "Zacchaeus"—He called him by name—"come down out of that tree. I'm going to go to your house today" (see Luke 19:5).

When Jesus called Zacchaeus down from that tree, it was a personal call. He used Zacchaeus' name. He said, "Zacchaeus, come down. I'm coming to your house."

All through history God has been calling people personally. Jesus said that He is the Good Shepherd, that the Good Shepherd *"calls his own sheep by name and leads them out"* (John 10:3).

In Genesis 3, we read that God came to the Garden of Eden personally and called, "Adam, Adam, where are you?" (See Genesis 3:9.) God knew where Adam was, but He wanted

Adam to know where he was—that he was separated from God by sin. And that sin is passed on from generation to generation until all of us are separated from God.

God called the Prophet Samuel by name. He called the Prophet Jeremiah by name. He called His disciples by name: Andrew and Peter, James and John. He called a tax collector named Matthew. On the Damascus Road He called a man named Saul and changed his name to Paul, and Paul became the greatest preacher in the history of the Church.

Jesus calls you and me by name: "Billy, Mary, Tyler, Hannah, John, I'm calling you to make a commitment in your life to Me. I want to bring new joy and peace and patience. I want to give you the absolute assurance that you are saved and that you are going to Heaven." It is a personal call. God knows everything about you.

Prayer *for the* Day:

Thank You, Heavenly Father, that You know me and called me by name, just as You called Zacchaeus. You know my thoughts, my sorrows and my joys. Give me Your peace, joy and patience as I seek to serve You today.

Day 20

I have set before you life and death, blessing and curse. Therefore choose life, that you and your offspring may live, loving the Lord your God, obeying his voice and holding fast to him, for he is your life and length of days. —DEUTERONOMY 30:19–20

God's View *of* Tolerance

One of the pet words of this age is "tolerance." It is a good word, but we have tried to stretch it over too great an area of life. Too often we have applied tolerance where it does not belong. The word "tolerant" means "broad-minded, willing to put up with beliefs opposed to one's convictions, the allowance of something not wholly approved."

Tolerance, in one sense, implies the compromise of one's convictions, a yielding of ground on important issues. Hence, over-tolerance in moral issues has made us soft, flabby and devoid of conviction.

We have become tolerant about divorce; we have become

tolerant about the use of alcohol; we have become tolerant about immorality; we have become tolerant about crime; and we have become tolerant about godlessness.

There is a manifest tolerance of broad-mindedness about morals; this is characteristic of our day. We have been sapped of our conviction and drained of our beliefs, and we are bereft of our faith.

If you were to ask someone the way to New York City and he said, "Oh, just take any road you wish," you would question either his sanity or his truthfulness. Nevertheless, we have somehow gotten it into our minds that "all roads lead to Heaven." People say, "Do your best," "Be honest," and, "Be sincere—and you will make it to Heaven all right."

Jesus Christ, who journeyed from Heaven to earth and back to Heaven again, knew the way better than anyone who ever lived. He said, *"The gate is narrow and the way is hard that leads to life, and those who find it are few"* (Matthew 7:14).

Prayer *for the* Day:

Dear Lord, You have called me to the narrow path that leads to life. Give me strength to endure when I am tempted to turn aside. Help me not to allow the world's idea of tolerance to compromise my own convictions based on Your Word.

There is salvation in no one else [but Jesus], for there is no other name under heaven given among men by which we must be saved.
—ACTS 4:12

The Narrow Way *of* Salvation

People plead for broad-mindedness, tolerance and charity. Ambassadors use all of their powers to influence warring parties to come to the conference table in a spirit of give-and-take.

There is a sense in which the world needs broad-mindedness and tolerance, and certainly we all need understanding and charity. However, in the realm of Christian experience there is a need for intolerance in certain areas.

Once, while on a plane traveling to Japan, we flew through a rough snowstorm. When we arrived over the airport in Tokyo, the visibility was almost zero. The pilot had to make an instrument landing. I did not want that pilot to be broad-minded. I wanted him to be narrow-minded. I knew that our lives depended on it.

In some things Jesus Christ was the most tolerant, broad-minded Person who ever lived—but in other things He was one of the most intolerant. His was the intolerance of a pilot who maneuvers a plane through a storm, realizing that a single error, just one flash of broad-mindedness, might bring disaster to all those on the plane.

Christ was so intolerant of our lost estate that He left His throne in Heaven, took on Himself the form of man, suffered at the hands of evil men and died on a cruel cross to purchase our redemption. So serious was our plight that He could not look on it lightly. With the love that was His, He could not be broad-minded about a world held captive by its lusts, its appetites and its sins.

The Apostle Peter reflected Christ's teaching when he said, *"There is salvation in no one else"* (Acts 4:12). The Apostle Paul taught the same: *"There is one God, and there is one mediator between God and men, the man Christ Jesus"* (1 Timothy 2:5).

Prayer *for the* Day:

Your love, Lord Jesus, is available to all, and I am grateful. Help me to show Your tolerance to people but to be willing to stand firmly for truth, so that no one I know will be misled into eternal disaster.

*Jesus said to him, "If you would be perfect, go, sell what you possess and give to the poor, and you will have treasure in heaven; and come, follow me." —*MATTHEW 19:21

Intolerance *toward* Selfishness

Many of us suffer from spiritual nearsightedness. Our interests and our energies are too often focused on ourselves. Jesus said, *"If anyone would come after me, let him deny himself and take up his cross daily and follow me"* (Luke 9:23).

Jesus was intolerant of selfishness. To the rich young ruler He said, *"If you want to be perfect, go, sell what you possess and give to the poor, and you will have treasure in heaven"* (Matthew 19:21). It wasn't the giving of the man's goods that Jesus demanded, but his release from selfishness and its devastating effects on his personality and his life.

Jesus said, *"For whoever desires to save his life will lose it, but whoever loses his life for My sake will find it"* (Matthew 16:25, NKJV). Jesus was intolerant of selfishness, and the life that He urges us to lose is the selfishness that lives within us, the old nature of sin that is in conflict with God.

Peter, James and John left their nets, but Jesus did not object to nets as such; it was the selfish living that the nets symbolized that He wanted them to forsake. Matthew left a political job to follow Christ. But Jesus did not object to a political career as such; it was the selfish living that it represented that He wanted Matthew to forsake.

So, in your life and in my life, self must be crucified and Christ enthroned. Jesus was intolerant of any other way, for He knew that selfishness and the Holy Spirit of God cannot exist together.

Prayer *for the* Day:

Forgive me, Jesus, when I focus on myself instead of on others and on You. Give me the strength today to set aside my needs and desires and to devote my life to following You.

For God so loved the world, that he gave his only Son, that whoever believes in him should not perish but have eternal life.
—JOHN 3:16

Fighting Fire

Forest rangers know the value of backfires in fighting forest fires. To save an area from uncontrolled fire, fire fighters carefully burn away the trees and shrubs to create a fireline or safety barrier. When the forest fire reaches that burned-out area, plants and animals on the other side of the fireline are protected from the flames. Fire is thus fought with fire.

Calvary was a colossal fighting of fire with fire. Jesus Christ, taking on Himself all of our sins, allowed the fire of sin's judgment to fall on Him. The area at the cross is a place of refuge for all who would escape the judgment of sin.

Jesus was tolerant toward the sinner, but intolerant toward the evil that enslaves the sinner. To the adulteress He said,

"Neither do I condemn you; go, and from now on sin no more" (John 8:11). He forgave her, but He condemned her sin because He loathed it with holy hatred.

Christ was so intolerant toward sin that He died on the cross to free men and women from its power. Sin lies at the root of most of society's difficulties today. Whatever separates a person from God separates that person from others. The world problem will never be solved until the problem of sin is settled.

God is intolerant toward sin. That intolerance sent His Son to die for us. He has said that *"whoever believes in him is not condemned"* and that those who refuse to believe in Him will be eternally lost (see John 3:18).

The cross is God's solution to sin. To all who will receive the blessed news of salvation through Christ, the cross cancels forever sin's power.

Prayer *for the* Day:

You, God, have provided a refuge for sinners. Thank You for showing me my need for You, and providing rescue from my sins. Make Yourself known through my life so that others can share in the joy and peace You have given me.

No temptation has overtaken you that is not common to man. God is faithful, and he will not let you be tempted beyond your ability, but with the temptation he will also provide the way of escape.
—1 CORINTHIANS 10:13

Strength *to* Say "No"

More than 100 years ago a man was converted to Christ and became pastor of a church in the slums of London. He went to the poor and the down-and-out and the oppressed. He formed a little group called the Hallelujah Band, and he would stand on street corners and preach the Gospel.

Many of the clergy who knew him were embarrassed by it all. When he was called before a conference of religious leaders, they said, "William Booth, will you go where we tell you to go? If not, you will be defrocked." In the balcony his wife, Catherine, stood. She said, "William, say, 'No, never!'" And he said "no." That "no" changed history in Great Britain and in many other parts of the world. Booth did not give up and founded a new organization. Wherever The Salvation Army has gone, it has given help for the body and for the soul.

Vashti was queen of Persia and the wife of Xerxes (Ahasuerus), who reigned over territory from India to Ethiopia (see Esther 1:3–19). Xerxes gave a feast for the various princes and governors and leaders of the entire country. Toward the end of the feast, as Xerxes became drunk, he ordered Vashti, his wife, to come to the feast. She sent word back and said, "No, I will not come."

Vashti was ready to give up every luxury that she had to keep herself pure. She would not expose her body, would not degrade her character.

When we say "no," God will help us to stand by it. He will give us courage. You say, "But the temptations are so great. I can't resist them." Of course, you can't. In my own strength I can't either. We cannot live pure lives without the help of God. We need to let Jesus Christ help us to resist temptation.

Prayer *for the* Day:

Dear Jesus, be my strength when I am tempted. Help me to say "no" to the allures of the world and to say "yes" to Your will for my life.

48

But Daniel resolved that he would not defile himself with the king's food, or with the wine that he drank. —DANIEL 1:8

A Dangerous Refusal

Daniel was a young man who had found purpose in life. As a teenager, he had been captured by the Babylonians. He was taken to Babylon to be trained in all their ways. But Daniel refused to eat the king's meat or drink the king's wine even though he knew how dangerous that refusal was.

Daniel was a long way from home. He could have yielded; no one back home would have known the difference. Daniel knew that it might mean death to refuse the king. This early "no" in Daniel's life prepared him to refuse the gifts that Belshazzar promised him if he would interpret the writing on the wall (see Daniel 5:16–17).

We defile ourselves. How? By eating too much; drinking too much alcohol; taking drugs; watching too many movies that are wrong; watching too much television.

In Luke 21 we read, *"Watch yourselves lest your hearts be weighed down with dissipation and drunkenness and cares of this life, and that day come upon you suddenly like a trap"* (Luke 21:34). What day? We know that there is a day coming in which we will have to give an account before God at the Judgment, because God is a God of judgment.

If we take a stand and mean it, we may suffer persecution. Some of our friends may drift away. They won't want to be with people like us. We speak to their consciences. They may feel uncomfortable in our presence because we live for God. Jesus said, *"Blessed are you when people hate you and when they exclude you and revile you and spurn your name as evil, on account of the Son of Man! Rejoice in that day, and leap for joy, for behold, your reward is great in heaven"* (Luke 6:22–23).

Prayer *for the* Day:

Father, You know my heart. Keep me from defiling myself by giving in to my own desires. Let me be a positive influence for You in all that I do.

Day 26

[Moses] considered the reproach of Christ greater wealth than the treasures of Egypt, for he was looking to the reward.
—HEBREWS 11:26

Pleasure *or* Joy?

Moses had to make a choice, just as we have to make choices. The Bible says, *"By faith Moses, when he was grown up, refused to be called the son of Pharaoh's daughter, choosing rather to be mistreated with the people of God than to enjoy the fleeting pleasures of sin"* (Hebrews 11:24–25).

As heir to the throne of Egypt, Moses had the choice of accepting all the pleasures of Egypt.

But one day he made a choice. Moses said "no" to all that was offered. He said, "I'll go suffer with the people of God. I choose God rather than these pleasures."

There is a difference between pleasure and joy. The Bible says, *"Whoever loves pleasure will be a poor man"* (Proverbs 21:17). When we love pleasure, we are poor, if that is what we are seeking.

51

Scripture talks about *"lovers of pleasure rather than lovers of God"* (2 Timothy 3:4). Do you love pleasure more than you love God?

Joy is produced by the Holy Spirit. When we come to Jesus Christ, the Holy Spirit comes to dwell in our hearts. More than 100 Scriptures talk about the joy of the Lord. That was the announcement at that first Christmas: *"Fear not. ... I bring you good news of great joy that will be for all the people"* (Luke 2:10).

Jesus said, *"Rejoice that your names are written in heaven"* (Luke 10:20). Make the choice that Moses made—he turned his back on pleasure and followed God's way.

The Scriptures say, *"Count it all joy ... when you meet trials of various kinds"* (James 1:2). Moses chose the joy of following God rather than having the pleasures of Egypt.

Prayer *for the* Day:

Dear Lord, You have offered me the joy of Your salvation, and I thank You for that. Today may I choose to follow You in all I do rather than choosing the pleasures of this world.

Day 27

In this the love of God was made manifest among us, that God sent his only Son into the world, so that we might live through him.
—1 JOHN 4:9

The Wonder *of* God's Love

There were seven wonders of the ancient world, and I have read of the seven wonders of the modern world. But God has His seven wonders too. The first is the wonder of His love. Almighty God, who is from everlasting to everlasting, the Creator of the whole universe, loves you and is interested in you, as if you were the only person who ever lived. He loves you so much that He gave His only Son for you.

Loneliness is one of the greatest problems that people face. We can be in a crowd, we can be at a party, and we can all of a sudden feel lonely. That is loneliness for God. We were made for fellowship with God. That fellowship has been broken by sin, and so we are lonely for God. We don't find fulfillment or purpose or meaning in life because we are without God.

That is why Christ came—to bring us to God. God gave His Son to die on the cross to save us. God says, *"I have loved you with an everlasting love"* (Jeremiah 31:3).

Jesus Christ loved us from the cross where He shed His blood for us: *"the blood of Jesus his Son cleanses us from all sin"* (1 John 1:7). That is the only cleansing power that will wash away sin—the blood of Christ which was shed on the cross for you. If you turn away from His love, there is no hope. When we are away from God, when we are sinning against God and we have broken God's laws and we have disobeyed Him, He still wants to put His arms around us and say, "I love you." From the cross God is saying to us, "I love you."

Prayer *for the* Day:

Thank You, dear Jesus, for loving me enough to die for me. When I fail You, draw me back to Your side and remind me of that everlasting love.

Day 28

When the fullness of the time had come, God sent forth His Son, born of a woman. —GALATIANS 4:4, NKJV

Where *is* God?

The second of God's wonders is the wonder of God coming to live among us: *"The Word became flesh and dwelt among us"* (John 1:14). That is a tremendous thing. It means that the whole of everything that we can think of came to dwell among us. God became a man. He became flesh so that He might experience our temptations and be tempted as we are. He understands us.

When I was speaking at Harvard University one time, a student told me the story of a little girl who came home from Sunday school and asked, "Mommy, where is God?"

"Oh, darling," replied her mother, "God is everywhere."

The little girl said, "But I don't want God to be everywhere. I want God to be somewhere, and I want Him to be somebody."

Since mankind's fall in the Garden of Eden, God has revealed

Himself in history. God chose a man, Abraham, who became a great nation. God miraculously delivered His chosen people from Egypt. Under Moses' leadership the people crossed the Red Sea. God gave them the Ten Commandments, and He gave Israel prophets whose divinely inspired predictions were absolutely trustworthy.

But most of all, God revealed Himself in the Person of His Son, Jesus Christ: *"No one has ever seen God, but the one and only Son, who is himself God and is in closest relationship with the Father, has made him known"* (John 1:18, NIV).

God is in Christ. When I see the love of Christ feeding the 5,000, bringing the dead to life, making the blind to see and the lame to walk, I see God and His love and compassion for us.

Prayer *for the* Day:

Dear God, I am overwhelmed when I think about You leaving Heaven to come to earth for my sake. Work through my life to show Your love and truth to people I know.

Day 29

[God] made Him who knew no sin to be sin for us, that we might become the righteousness of God in Him.
—2 CORINTHIANS 5:21, NKJV

My Sins *are* Gone

The third of God's wonders is the wonder of the cross. We can never understand the depths of this wonder. *"My God, my God, why have you forsaken me?"* (Matthew 27:46) is the cry from the cross. What happened in that moment? Lightning crashed, thunder roared and darkness settled on the earth. Scripture says, *"The Lord has laid on him the iniquity of us all"* (Isaiah 53:6).

Jesus Christ was dying for you and for me. But He wasn't just dying the physical death from the nails in His hands and the spear in His side and the crown of thorns on His brow and the lashing of His back with a leather whip with steel pellets on the end. That was His physical suffering. But His spiritual suffering came when God laid on Him your sins and my sins. Scripture says He became sin for us. He became guilty of adultery, murder, lust, greed, pride and everything that you can think of. He had never known sin, but He took the penalty for all our sin.

He became sin for us and took our guilt. He took the judgment and the hell that we deserve. The Bible says, *"The wages of sin is death"* (Romans 6:23). That means judgment and hell. I deserve judgment. I am a sinner. I have broken God's Law. I deserve the judgment that is coming to me. But instead of that judgment striking me, it struck Christ. That is what the cross is all about. That is why the cross is the great symbol of Christianity. But Jesus didn't stay on the cross. He rose from the dead. He is alive, and He is coming again.

How wonderful to know that my sins are gone. *"There is therefore now no condemnation for those who are in Christ Jesus"* (Romans 8:1).

Prayer *for the* Day:

What a wonderful Savior You are, Jesus. You have taken my guilt and my shame and made me new. Let me be Your witness to those around me who are dead in sin. I want them to know You died so that they can live.

Unless you are converted and become as little children, you will by no means enter the kingdom of heaven. —MATTHEW 18:3, NKJV

From Old *to* New

The fourth wonder is the wonder of conversion. Jesus said you cannot enter the Kingdom of Heaven unless you are converted. The word "converted" confuses some people because it has been misused so many times. We think we have to have great emotion, that we have to do this and we have to do that, that lightning has to strike or something has to happen. Rather, we are asked to say "no" to sin and "yes" to Christ. The word "conversion" means to change, to turn. It implies to turn from something toward something else. *"Therefore, if anyone is in Christ, he is a new creation. The old has passed away; behold, the new has come"* (2 Corinthians 5:17).

Something new comes, and it is accomplished by the Holy Spirit. You cannot convert yourself. You have to have God to help you to repent. You need to confess your sin and turn from it, putting your faith and total confidence in Christ.

People come to Christ in different ways. I came to Christ very simply. I remember that I was a member of the church, vice president of the young people's society in our church, and I thought I was all right. Everybody considered me to be a good boy. But down deep in my heart I knew there was something missing.

But one night I went to an evangelistic meeting. I went several nights, and the Spirit of God spoke to me and I gave my heart to Jesus Christ. The next day I knew that something had happened. I didn't know what, but I knew I was different. I began to want to read the Bible and I wanted to go to church. That simple act of saying "yes" to Christ changed my life.

Prayer *for the* Day:

Yes, Lord, I have given You my heart and my life. Continue the work that You have begun in my life. Through Your Holy Spirit, convict others of their need to repent and be changed.

Peace I leave with you; my peace I give to you. Not as the world gives do I give to you. Let not your hearts be troubled, neither let them be afraid. —JOHN 14:27

Peace, Hope, *and* Faith

The fifth wonder is the gift of peace and joy that Christ gives. Jesus said, *"Peace I leave with you; my peace I give to you"* (John 14:27). Do you have peace in your heart? Do you have joy? The wonder of God's love and the forgiveness He offers through Jesus Christ brings peace and joy.

The sixth wonder is God's plan for the future: *"our blessed hope, the appearing of the glory of our great God and Savior Jesus Christ"* (Titus 2:13). I look for Him all the time—for that day when He will return. What a glorious day that will be when we see Him face to face.

The seventh wonder is your own commitment to Jesus Christ. Jesus Christ has come to save you, but He won't force you to make that commitment. It is voluntary. He won't make anyone come to Him.

A prominent church official says that what is principally wrong with the church is that too often we have been trying to get people to act like Christians when they have never committed their lives to Christ. We want them to act like Christians, but they have no capacity to be Christians because Christ doesn't live in their hearts.

In a world at war, with trouble and revolution and terrorism, you can have peace. In a world of hatred, you can have love. In a doubting world, you can have faith, when Jesus Christ lives in Your heart.

Prayer *for the* Day:

My heart is full, O God, because of the peace, hope and faith You give me. Show that peace and hope to the world through my actions of love. Help me not to judge people who do not know You, but to tell them about Your unfailing love.

Sources

"You Cannot Be Neutral," *Decision* magazine, September 1986: What is a Christian?, Choosing Your Road, No Compromise, Has your Life been Transformed?, Neutral is Not an Option

"The Only Way," *Decision* magazine, August 1997: The Only Way

"The Only Way," *Decision* magazine, August 1997 and "Jesus Is Who He Said He Is," *Decision* magazine, July–August 1985: Truth Does Not Change

"New Heart, New Beginning," *Decision* magazine, January 1997: New Heart, New Beginning; Dye on Our Souls; Two Greatest Words

"God's View of Tolerance," *Decision* magazine, July 1998: Two Roads in Life, God's View of Tolerance, The Narrow Way of Salvation, Intolerance toward Selfishness, Fighting Fire

"You Cannot Be Neutral," *Decision* magazine, September 1986 and "The Only Way," Decision magazine, August 1997: You Can Depend on the Bible

"Jesus Is Who He Said He Is," *Decision* magazine, July–August 1985: The Word Has Power, He is who He Said

"What Is Truth?," *Decision* magazine, February 1985: What Is Truth?, Truth or Lies?, Like Little Children

"He Calls Us By Name," *Decision* magazine, July 1996: Obstacles to Jesus, He Calls Us by Name

"Strength to Say 'No,'" *Decision* magazine, May 1994: Strength to Say "No," A Dangerous Refusal, Pleasure or Joy?

"God's Seven Wonders," *Decision* magazine, July–August 1986: The Wonder of God's Love; My Sins are Gone; From Old to New; Peace, Hope, and Faith

"God's Seven Wonders," *Decision* magazine, July–August 1986 and "The Only Way," *Decision* magazine, August 1997: Where is God?

Steps to Peace with God

STEP 1   God's Purpose: Peace and Life

God loves you and wants you to experience peace and life—abundant and eternal.

THE BIBLE SAYS ...

"We have peace with God through our Lord Jesus Christ."
Romans 5:1

Since God planned for us to have peace and the abundant life right now, why are most people not having this experience?

"For God so loved the world that He gave His only begotten Son, that whoever believes in Him should not perish but have everlasting life."
John 3:16, NKJV

"I have come that they may have life, and that they may have it more abundantly." *John 10:10, NKJV*

STEP 2 Our Problem: Separation from God

God created us in His own image to have an abundant life. He did not make us as robots to automatically love and obey Him, but gave us a will and a freedom of choice.

We chose to disobey God and go our own willful way. We still make this choice today. This results in separation from God.

THE BIBLE SAYS ...

"For all have sinned and fall short of the glory of God." *Romans 3:23*

"For the wages of sin is death, but the free gift of God is eternal life in Christ Jesus our Lord." *Romans 6:23*

Our choice results in separation from God.

People (Sinful)

God (Holy)

Our Attempts

Through the ages, individuals have tried in many ways to bridge this gap ... without success ...

THE BIBLE SAYS ...

"There is a way that seems right to a man, but its end is the way to death." *Proverbs 14:12*

"But your iniquities have separated you from your God; and your sins have hidden His face from you, so that He will not hear." *Isaiah 59:2, NKJV*

There is only one remedy for this problem of separation.

STEP 3 God's Remedy: The Cross

Jesus Christ is the only answer to this problem. He died on the cross and rose from the grave, paying the penalty for our sin and bridging the gap between God and people.

THE BIBLE SAYS ...

"For there is one God, and there is one mediator between God and men, the man Christ Jesus." *1 Timothy 2:5*

"For Christ also suffered once for sins, the just for the unjust, that He might bring us to God." *1 Peter 3:18, NKJV*

"But God demonstrates His own love toward us, in that while we were still sinners, Christ died for us." *Romans 5:8, NKJV*

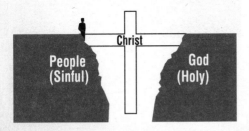

God has provided the only way ... we must make the choice ...

STEP 4   Our Response: Receive Christ

We must trust Jesus Christ and receive Him by personal invitation ...

THE BIBLE SAYS ...

"Behold, I stand at the door and knock. If anyone hears My voice and opens the door, I will come in to him and dine with him, and he with Me." *Revelation 3:20, NKJV*

"But as many as received Him, to them He gave the right to become children of God, to those who believe in His name." *John 1:12, NKJV*

"If you confess with your mouth the Lord Jesus and believe in your heart that God has raised Him from the dead, you will be saved." *Romans 10:9, NKJV*

Are you here ...   *or here?*

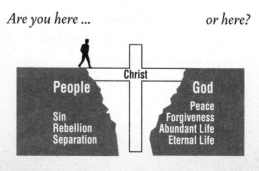

Is there any good reason why you cannot receive
Jesus Christ right now?

How to receive Christ:

1. Admit your need (I am a sinner).
2. Be willing to turn from your sins (repent) and ask for God's forgiveness.
3. Believe that Jesus Christ died for you on the cross and rose from the grave.
4. Through prayer, invite Jesus Christ to come in and control your life through the Holy Spirit (receive Jesus as Lord and Savior).

What to Pray:

Dear Lord Jesus,

I know that I am a sinner, and I ask for Your forgiveness. I believe You died for my sins and rose from the dead. I turn from my sins and invite You to come into my heart and life. I want to trust and follow You as my Lord and Savior.

In Your Name, amen.

_____   _____
Date   Signature

God's Assurance: His Word

If you prayed this prayer,

THE BIBLE SAYS ...

"For 'everyone who calls on the name of the Lord will be saved.'" *Romans 10:13*

Did you sincerely ask Jesus Christ to come into your life? Where is He right now? What has He given you?

"For by grace you have been saved through faith. And this is not your own doing; it is the gift of God, not a result of works, so that no one may boast." *Ephesians 2:8–9*

The Bible Says ...

"He who has the Son has life; he who does not have the Son of God does not have life. These things I have written to you who believe in the name of the Son of God, that you may know that you have eternal life, and that you may continue to believe in the name of the Son of God." *1 John 5:12–13, NKJV*

Receiving Christ, we are born into God's family through the supernatural work of the Holy Spirit who indwells every believer. This is called regeneration or the "new birth."

This is just the beginning of a wonderful new life in Christ. To deepen this relationship, you should:

1. Read your Bible every day to know Christ better.
2. Talk to God in prayer every day.
3. Tell others about Christ.
4. Worship, fellowship, and serve with other Christians in a church where Christ is preached.
5. As Christ's representative in a needy world, demonstrate your new life by your love and concern for others.

God bless you as you do.
Billy Graham

If you are committing your life to Christ, please let us know!
We would like to send you Bible study materials to help you grow in
your faith.

The Billy Graham Evangelistic Association exists to support and extend
the evangelistic calling and ministries of Billy Graham and Franklin
Graham by proclaiming the Gospel of the Lord Jesus Christ to all we can
by every effective means available to us and by equipping others to do
the same.

Our desire is to introduce as many people as we can to the person of
Jesus Christ, so that they might experience His love and forgiveness.
Your prayers are the most important way to support us in this ministry.
We are grateful for the dedicated prayer support we receive. We are also
grateful for those who support us with financial contributions.

Billy Graham Evangelistic Association
1 Billy Graham Parkway
Charlotte, North Carolina 28201-0001
BillyGraham.org
Toll-free: 1-877-2GRAHAM
(1-877-247-2426)

Billy Graham Evangelistic Association of Canada
20 Hopewell Way NE
Calgary, Alberta T3J 5H5
BillyGraham.ca
Toll-free: 1-888-393-0003